CONTENTS

Chap. 17 Stare

RYO-KUN, THE DESIGNER, IS TRANSGENDER, AND WORRIES ABOUT THE DISCONNECT BETWEEN HOW HE IDENTIFIES AND HIS PHYSICAL SEX.

IN OTHER WORDS, HIS BODY IS FEMALE, BUT IN HIS HEART, HE'S MALE.

...WHA...?

!

ブ゛゛
ブ゛
ブ゛゛
VRRR

WHAT ARE THEY DOING...?

WHY...?

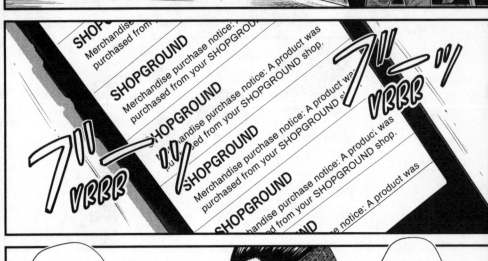

DRIP...

...WATARI-SAN!

HEY... WE'RE IN THE SAME CLASS...

PAT

FLINCH

...!

BA-DUMP

IT'S AMAZING!!

GLAMOR

!!

WE SAW YOUR FASHION BRAND!

IT'S SO AWESOME!!

I BOUGHT A SHIRT!

YOU'RE GOING SUPER VIRAL!

ARE YOU FRIENDS WITH WING-KUN?!

NO SKIRT, EITHER.

I KNOW.

...WOW, YEAH, THAT'S A JERSEY.

!!

REALLY? SO...

YEAH, THAT KID IS, UH...

I'VE SEEN THEIR FACE EVERYWHERE.

QUEER?

...W-WATARI-SAN!

...

WE'RE NOT GONNA JUDGE YOU!

RIGHT?

YEAH!

IT'S OKAY! WE DON'T CARE!

...

...BUT, Y'KNOW...

...

...YEAH.

...! *CHIKA*...

WATARI-SAN AND HIS FRIENDS WERE IN WING-KUN'S VIDEO!!

I THINK HE *DEFINITELY* HAS A CRUSH ON YOU, TOO.

I WONDER WHY HE NEVER TOLD YOU, EVEN THOUGH YOU TWO ARE SO CLOSE...

THINK ABOUT WHAT IT'S BEEN LIKE SHARING THE GIRLS' BATHROOM AND LOCKER ROOM WITH HIM ALL THIS TIME.

WELL, IF IT REALLY *IS* TRUE...

SO, OUR ONLY ABSENTEE IS...

...WATARI.

MUTTER

MUTTER

MUTTER

MUTTER

MUTTER

MUTTER

ALL RIGHT, EVERYONE, GET READY FOR FIRST PERIOD.

CAN YOU DELETE THAT VIDEO?

I'M SORRY, BUT...

WE ASKED YOU TO SHOW IT TO US FIRST.

IT WASN'T WHAT WE WERE EXPECTING.

Chap. 18 Extort

YOU SHARED HIS PRIVATE INFORMATION, AND EVEN A PICTURE OF HIM.

NOW TENS OF THOUSANDS OF PEOPLE HAVE SEEN IT.

WHAT'S THE POINT OF DELETING IT, ANYWAY?

!

...AND IT GETS YOU A LOT OF PUBLICITY.

THINGS GOT EASIER FOR ME WHEN I CAME OUT...

SHOWING YOU MY CLOSET #LGBTQ #FASHION

13,015 VIEWS

1398 25 SHARE SAVE ...

YOU HAVE TO USE EVERY TRICK IN THE BOOK—

...IT'S *YOUR CHOICE* IF YOU WANNA USE HIS STORY FOR YOUR PERSONAL GAIN.

BUT...

...THERE MUST BE A PART OF YOU THAT FEELS INCREDIBLY GUILTY OVER IT.

...

DON'T EXPECT OTHERS TO HAVE THE SAME KIND OF STRENGTH AS YOU.

IT'S NOT RIGHT AT ALL...!

IN FACT, IT'S COMPLETELY *WRONG!*

THIS ISN'T RIGHT ...!

...

WHAT ABOUT HOW *RYO* FEELS...?!

THERE'S NOT MUCH WE CAN DO ABOUT IT.

IT'S ALREADY DONE...

IN ANY CASE...

YOU ONLY MANAGED TO GET TO THIS POINT...

...YOU'RE NOT WRONG, TSUBASA-CHAN.

...BECAUSE YOU KNOW YOURSELF AND HAVE THE STRENGTH TO KEEP GOING FORWARD.

SORRY, I'M GOIN' HOME NOW.

WHAT ARE YOU UP TO NOW, CHIKA?

HIS BODY IS FEMALE, BUT IN HIS HEART, HE'S MALE.

...RYO-CHAN...

...SO MANY THINGS ABOUT YOU THAT I DIDN'T KNOW?

SINCE WHEN WERE THERE...

WHY DIDN'T HE TELL ME ANYTHING ABOUT IT...?!

HE'S SO SHY AND QUIET AND DOESN'T HAVE MANY FRIENDS...

I GOTTA FIND OUT, EVEN IF HE DOESN'T LIKE IT.

...SO I HAVE TO SUPPORT HIM...!!

THERE'S A CHICK WITH BRIGHT HAIR STANDIN' OUTSIDE OUR HOUSE...

HUH?

!

FWOOP

...

IS THAT GYARU GIRL YOUR FRIEND?

...WELL, IT'S ALREADY DONE NOW.

BUT...

WHAT?!

NO WAY! THAT'S ABSOLUTELY RIDICULOUS!

NO, I'M NOT.

THEY SHOWED A PHOTO OF ME WITHOUT MY PERMISSION...

BUT MOST PEOPLE WERE SURPRISINGLY KIND...

...WHEN I WENT TO SCHOOL...

...SOME PEOPLE SAID THEY'RE SCARED TO BE AROUND ME, OR TOOK PICTURES OF ME...

...BUT WHY DID IT BOTHER ME SO MUCH?

THEY WERE *TRYING* TO SAY NICE THINGS TO ME...

IT'S
OKAY.

Chap. 19 Growing Apart

IF PEOPLE KNOW NOW...

YOU NEED TO EXPLAIN IT TO THEM YOURSELF.

...IT'S NO GOOD IF THEY ONLY KNOW FROM THAT VIDEO.

...ESPECIALLY THOSE IMPORTANT TO YOU... LIKE YOUR FRIENDS...

...AND THAT GIRL YOU LIKE.

ANYWAY, I'LL TELL HER EVENTUALLY...

...BUT ALSO THE ONE I WANT TO UNDERSTAND ME THE MOST.

SHE'S THE ONE I WANNA TELL THE LEAST...

...HATING ME.

EVEN IF SHE ENDS UP...

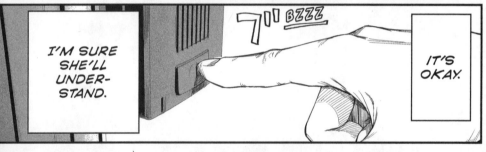

I'M SURE SHE'LL UNDER-STAND.

IT'S OKAY.

CHIKA!

AND WHAT IT SAID...

ABOUT THAT VIDEO...

IT'S... ACTUALLY TRUE!!

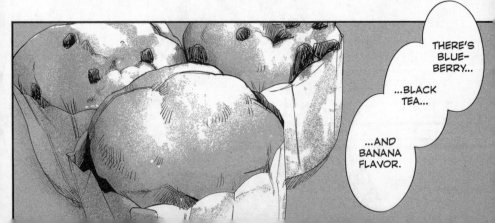

...THANK YOU.

...THIS FEELS KINDA NOSTALGIC.

YOU DON'T REALLY LIKE SWEET THINGS, DO YOU?

SO YOU CHOSE BLACK TEA, RYO-CHAN.

...YEAH, I DID.

JUST AS A FRIEND, THOUGH...

YOU ALWAYS GAVE ME STUFF ON VALENTINE'S DAY.

NOSTAL-GIC?

HUH?

WHY?

...THAT I GIVE YOU SOME.

BUT I WONDER IF MAYBE THIS SHOULD BE THE LAST TIME...

WHY DID YOU NEVER TELL ME ABOUT YOURSELF, RYO-CHAN?

ALL THIS TIME.

GULP

YOU'VE ALWAYS BEEN SO COOL...

UH...

...BUT REALLY, YOU'RE QUITE ENDEARING.

YOU WEREN'T THAT SOCIABLE AND KEPT AWAY FROM OTHERS...

...EVER SINCE WE MET...

...AND I WAS SO HAPPY THAT WE BECAME CLOSE. BUT...

IN MIDDLE SCHOOL, I TRIED TO TALK TO YOU AS MUCH AS I COULD...

WHAT IS SHE TALKING ABOUT...?

NO...

...I HAVE AN ILLNESS OR SOMETHING—

SHE'S TALKING JUST LIKE...

...HUH?

YOU KNOW, THAT BLONDE GIRL.

I FEEL FRUSTRATED WITH MYSELF... BUT I'M ALSO RELIEVED.

...IT'S COMPLICATED, ISN'T IT?

YOU WERE LEANING ON HER.

I SAW YOU WITH HER.

...DIDN'T KNOW ANYTHING ABOUT YOU, RYO-CHAN...

I...

SHE LOOKED SO CARING.

...YOU SHOULD TURN TO HER WHEN YOU NEED IT.

...BUT IF YOU HAVE SOMEONE WHO ACCEPTS YOU *LIKE THAT*...

BESIDES...
YOU SUIT
EACH
OTHER.

...EVEN THOUGH WE WERE ALWAYS SO CLOSE...

...I COULDN'T TELL HER A SINGLE THING.

I NEVER DID TELL HER ANYTHING, DID I?

...THAT STAYING SILENT ALL THIS TIME...

I NEVER EXPECTED...

...THAN THE REGRET OF NOT TELLING ANYONE.

...WOULD HURT LESS...

WHAT EXACTLY WAS I EVEN AFRAID OF?

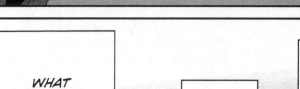

THE STARES?

...WAS IT THE RIDI-CULE?

CHATTER
ザワ

CHATTER
ザワ

JIN...!!

CHATTER
ザワ

2 - 1

I'LL
SAY IT
AS MANY
TIMES AS
YOU WANT
ME TO.

HEY,
SAY THAT
AGAIN.

SURE.

YOU'RE A CRAFTY LITTLE ASSHOLE.

YOU USED YOUR FRIEND TO TRY AND BUTTER UP THAT YOUTUBER, DIDN'T YOU?

NOW I UNDER- STAND.

NOW I KNOW WHY YOU BUDDIED UP TO WATARI!

WHAT?

Chap. 20 Indebtedness

EITHER YOU WERE USIN' HIM FOR SALES, OR JUST LOOKIN' FOR ATTENTION.

...IF YOU HAD SOMEONE LIKE *WATARI* WITH YOU, AFTER ALL.

IT'D BE MUCH EASIER TO GET CLOSE TO AN LGBTQ YOUTUBER...

...BY SAYIN' RYO IS QUEER, TOO.

THEY GOT CLOSE TO WING...

AH, I SEE... SO THAT'S WHY WATARI CAME OUT.

CHATTER...

I WONDER WHAT WATARI'S GONNA SHOW UP TO SCHOOL LOOKIN' LIKE!

ALL OF US...

...ARE SO CONFUSED, AREN'T WE?

AREN'T YOU ALL CURIOUS, TOO?

...

HMM.

WHEN YOU PUT IT LIKE THAT... YEAH.

HOW COULD WE *NOT BE*? YESTERDAY *SHE* WAS A *GIRL*, BUT NOW *HE* SAYS HE'S ACTUALLY A *BOY*.

SHOCK...

UH... WELL...

I DIDN'T MEAN IT LIKE *THAT*...

IS IT *REALLY* THAT UNAVOIDABLE?!

CHIHIRO'S RIGHT...

THE WAY THINGS ARE NOW, I DON'T BLAME RYO FOR NOT WANTING TO COME TO SCHOOL.

...OR THE RIGHT WAY TO INTERACT WITH HIM.

RYO NEVER FULLY EXPLAINED WHAT'S GOING ON WITH HIM...

BUT TO BE HONEST... I DON'T REALLY GET HIM, EITHER.

EVEN THOUGH THEY MADE FUN OF BOYS RUN THE RIOT...

WHY DIDN'T YOU SAY ANYTHING...?

JIN...!

...AND TALKED ABOUT RYO LIKE THAT?!

...HE'S NOT WRONG THAT I'M ALL TALK AT THE MOMENT.

WELL...

I FUCKED UP.

I THINK I'M AT FAULT FOR INVOLVING TSUBASA.

...'CUZ THEY DIDN'T THINK IT'S ANYTHING TO FEEL ASHAMED ABOUT.

...I GOT THE SENSE THAT MAYBE THEY OUTED RYO...

...BUT YESTERDAY, WHEN WE WERE TALKING WITH TSUBASA AND KASHIWABARA...

HE'S ONLY SUFFERIN' 'CUZ HE'S ASHAMED OF WHO HE IS.

THIS IS SOMETHIN' ONLY *HE* CAN OVERCOME.

...OR, "I RECOGNIZE YOU FOR WHO YOU ARE"...

SORRY, BUT I COULD NEVER SAY SOMETHING LIKE...

"SURE, IT AIN'T WEIRD"...

...

GLANCE...
チラ...

?

...NOW...

...WHAT
SHOULD
I DO...?

Chap. 21 Border

...EXCUSE ME, HINATA-SENSEI.

MAY I TELL EVERYONE SOMETHING...

...JUST FOR A MINUTE?

...OKAY.

WATARI...

I THOUGHT YOU MIGHT LET ME, AT THIS TIME OF DAY...

SO...

WE'RE IN THE MIDDLE OF CLASS.

...WELL, WHAT?

CHATTER

ARE YOU COSPLAYING OR SOME-THING?

CHATTER

...WHAT'S WITH THE BOYS' UNI-FORM?

AND WHY NOW?

WHAT'S GOIN' ON...?!

CHATTER

CHATTER

THEIR STARES ARE KILLING ME.

...JUST AS I THOUGHT.

...STILL...

...BUT...

...

YOU GOT THIS, RYO-CHAN!!

...ABOUT THAT VIDEO...

...FIRST...

...IS ALL TRUE.

WHAT WAS SAID IN THAT VIDEO...

...I FEEL UNCOMFORTABLE WEARING SKIRTS THAT LABEL ME AS A GIRL...

I WAS BORN FEMALE, AND I HAVE A FEMALE BODY.

HOWEVER...

I FEEL LIKE I'D PREFER TO HAVE A MALE BODY...

...AND I WANT TO BE ONE OF THE BOYS.

I'M SURE OF IT.

THAT'S HOW I TRULY FEEL.

...BECAUSE I LOOK LIKE A GIRL FROM THE OUTSIDE. IF I TOLD YOU THE TRUTH...

I DIDN'T TELL YOU UNTIL NOW...

...AND UNCOMFORTABLE.

...CURIOUS...

...CONCERNED...

...I WAS SURE YOU'D BE SHOCKED...

...

I WORE GIRLS' CLOTHES, AND WHEN WE WERE SPLIT BY GENDER, I'D GO TO THE GIRLS' SIDE.

...BUT THAT DIDN'T WORK.

SO I TRIED TO MAKE MY MIND MATCH MY BODY.

I NEED TO REPAY THE KINDNESS OF THOSE IMPORTANT TO ME WITH SOME HONESTY.

SO...

UH, CAN I ASK A QUESTION?

...

I WAS PROTECTING MYSELF, BUT I FAILED TO NOTICE THE PEOPLE WHO WERE DESPERATELY CONCERNED FOR ME.

ISN'T THIS ONLY HAPPENING 'CUZ YOU WANT ATTENTION?

I BET THE GOAL WAS TO BEFRIEND THAT POPULAR LGBTQ YOUTUBER FROM THE BEGINNING.

WHAT...?

DIDN'T YOU THINK IT WAS WEIRD?

THAT YOU AND JIN SUDDENLY BECAME SO CLOSE AND STARTED A FASHION BRAND.

MY POINT IS, I'M ALREADY TIRED OF THAT JOKE OF A BRAND OF YOURS.

THAT'S THE FIRST THING THAT STRUCK ME...

...ABOUT THAT VIDEO.

IT'S SO BORING. CAN YOU AT LEAST GO DO IT SOMEWHERE ELSE?

YOU'RE WELCOME TO PLAY PRETEND AT BEING FRIENDS, ENJOYIN' YOUR YOUTH...

...BUT IT'S A PRETTY FLIMSY FAÇADE.

...

AFTER ALL, YOU...

BONK

!

AH, OW!!

WHA...

K-KASHIWA-BARA...

WILL YOU SHUT UP ALREADY?

?!

HUH?

THAT WAS TOO HARSH.

YUP.

YEAH.

HE SURE IS MEAN, HUH?

WHAT'S WITH YOU ALL...?!

...

...JUST BY CHANGIN' YOUR UNIFORM?!

YOU THINK YOU CAN BECOME ONE OF THE GUYS...

...

DON'T YOU ALL AGREE?!

ONCE A GIRL, ALWAYS A GIRL!

FWIP

CLAMOR

NO, W—

WAIT—!

TUG

HUH?

CLOTHES HAVE THE POWER TO COMMUNICATE CERTAIN THINGS.

IT SAYS, "HEY, THIS PERSON IS A GIRL."

MY UNIFORM IS ANNOYING.

IT SPEAKS ON MY BEHALF.

...AND *EMPHASIZE* IT.

SO, I WANTED TO BORROW THAT POWER...

I'VE SUFFERED 'CUZ OF CLOTHES THAT HAVE CON-STRICTED ME...

...BUT THEY'VE ALSO ALLOWED ME TO *EXPRESS MY TRUE SELF.*

THE REASON I'M STARTING A FASHION BRAND...

I MET JIN...

IT'S OLD NEWS THAT I'M A WEIRDO WHO'S AWKWARD TO DEAL WITH.

GENDER XX

STEREO TYPE XY

...AND I MADE THIS DECISION...

...WITH MY OWN FREE WILL.

I...

YOU CAN THINK WHAT YOU LIKE.

DING
DONG
DING
DONG

GOOD-BYE, HINATA-SENSEI!

GET HOME SAFE, KIDS.

BOYS RUN

ボーイズ・ラン・ザ・ライオット

THE RIOT

BOYS RUN

ボーイズ・ラン・ザ・ライオット

THE RIOT

YEAH! I SAW.

WHAT DO YOU THINK...

HEY, DID YOU SEE...

...WATARI-SAN?

Chap. 22 Revolution

YOU'RE NOT IN-TRIGUED AT ALL?

AS LONG AS IT SUITS HIM.

HMM, I DON'T REALLY MIND.

...OF HIS UNI-FORM?

NOT EXACTLY? BUT...

ART PREP ROOM

Photography Club Room

...IF I WAS CLOSER TO HIM, I MIGHT BE A BIT CONFUSED.

YEAH, TRUE.

...I'LL HAVE TO COME OUT TO MY FAMILY, TOO...

I KNOW THAT IF THIS KEEPS UP...

...SHUT UP.

WHAT HAPPENED WITH THAT, IN THE END?

...ANYWAY, ABOUT OUR SALES...

...WELL, WE SOLD APPROXI- MATELY...

ABOUT 20 TO 30 ITEMS, I BET!

WE SOLD QUITE A LOT, DIDN'T WE?

...350.

WE'VE MADE A PROFIT OF ABOUT... 1 MILLION YEN.

*Approximately $9,000 USD

...A MILLION...?!

A...

TSUBASA'S VIDEO DEFINITELY TRANSLATED INTO SALES.

WELL, IT'S NOT *THAT* MUCH WHEN YOU LOOK AT HOW MANY FOLLOWERS WING HAS, BUT AT LEAST SOME OF THEM FORKED OUT SOME CASH...

ALL FOR OUR CLOTHES.

...

WHAM

THEREFORE!

I PROPOSE WE HAVE A MEETING!!

I GUESS HE WANTS TO MAKE IT FEEL LIKE A REAL MEETING.

HE'S EVEN GOT DOCUMENTS.

SHWP

...

TAP

...THESE ARE SOME OF THE COMMENTS WE GOT ON OUR INSTAGRAM.

AND THAT'S THE TRUTH.

WE *DEFINITELY* GOT SALES...

...TO ALL THOSE FOLLOW-ERS...

...AND MORE PEOPLE GOT THE CHANCE TO SEE OUR CLOTHES.

WE GOT A LOT OF TRAFFIC AFTER TSUBASA INTRODUCED US...

...LET'S REVIEW.

...WHAT DO YOU GUYS THINK?

...

SO...

WHY ARE WE RUNNIN' THIS BRAND?

WHAT ARE...

...OUR MOTIVA-TIONS?

...I FULLY UNDER-STOOD...

...WHY I'M DOING THIS.

I THINK TODAY...

I GOT INVOLVED WITH FASHION IN ORDER TO LIVE AS A GUY.

...I WANNA DO THINGS DIFFERENTLY.

BUT...

I KNOW HOW INCREDIBLE TSUBASA IS MORE THAN ANYONE.

...FOR MONEY, EITHER.

I'M NOT REALLY DOING IT...

IT'S AN INSULT...

...TO OUR CLOTHING.

I DON'T WANNA USE MY COMING OUT AS OUR SELLIN' POINT.

IT MIGHT SEEM SILLY, BUT THAT'S IT, REALLY.

RIGHT NOW, I JUST REALLY WANNA TAKE PHOTOS OF YOUR BRAND MOST OF ALL.

NOT JUST CLOTHES MARKETED...

...TO TSUBASA'S FANS.

BUT I WANNA TAKE PICTURES OF COOL CLOTHES.

...

YOU'RE SO FUCKIN' IDEALISTIC.

IF WE DON'T USE WHATEVER OPPORTUNITIES WE GET, WE'LL JUST BE FORGOTTEN.

...

THIS IS OUR CHANCE TO GET PEOPLE'S ATTENTION, NO MATTER HOW.

...WHOEVER SELLS, WINS.

EVEN IF PEOPLE SHAME US OR TALK ABOUT US BEHIND OUR BACKS...

BUT...

...YOU DID IT, RYO.

HUH?

PANT

...

PANT

PANT

THEY CHANGED THE RULES.

...CHANGED THE WHOLE ATMOSPHERE IN THE CLASS-ROOM.

THE OTHER DAY, YOUR CLOTHES...

IT WAS REVOLUTIONARY.

LET'S MAKE A FRESH START.

ALL RIGHT!

...BUT THAT'S WHERE WE'LL START.

TSUBASA WON'T DELETE A VIDEO ONCE IT'S OUT...

IF WE HAVE A PROPER CONVERSA- TION...

...I'M SURE WE'LL GET THROUGH TO TSUBASA.

YEAH!

RYO? IN THE BOYS' UNIFORM?

HE'S QUITE THE DAREDEVIL.

THAT'S HOW HE DECIDED TO EXPRESS HIMSELF.

HAHA, NOPE!

...AND GO TO SCHOOL IN A SKIRT, DID YOU, TSUBASA-CHAN?

EVEN *YOU* DIDN'T IGNORE THE RULES...

HE SEEMED WORRIED ABOUT THE VIDEO AT ONE POINT...

HE'S VERY STRONG-WILLED.

HE'S COOL, ISN'T HE?

LOOKS LIKE IT ALL TURNED OUT FINE AFTER ALL.

...BUT NOW IT SEEMS LIKE HE'S GOTTEN OVER IT.

OH! YEAH.

DID THE OFFICE ALSO SAY THE VIDEO GOT A GOOD RESPONSE?

IF I EVER SHOWED MY TRUE COLORS, I'D GET BULLIED.

PEOPLE SAID A LOT OF HORRIBLE THINGS TO ME.

BEING AT SCHOOL WAS THE WORST. IT WAS HELL.

CONFESSIONAL

Chap. 23 Scandal

...BUT I NEVER HAVE.

I TRIED TO, REALLY, BUT IT WAS IMPOSSIBLE.

CONFESSIONAL

I'M OFTEN ASKED IF I'VE EVER FALLEN IN LOVE WITH A GIRL...

...

HIKE

what a cool way to live. it's beautiful, regardless of gender

  REPLY

MAKIRON

You stayed true to yourself no matter how hard it got, I respect that

  REPLY

▼ VIEW REPLIES

MAA

i love ur serious videos too!

  REPLY

AND OF COURSE, I'VE NEVER DONE ANYTHING SEXUAL WITH ONE, EITHER.

Looking back on my life being raised as a "boy"

958,168 VIEWS

634 COMMENTS

HEY, BOSS.

YOU CALLED?

OH, TSUBASA! YOU'RE HERE.

KER-CHAK

OH, DEAR.

I TOLD HIM TO BE CAREFUL, DAMMIT...

HE SLEPT WITH A FAN AND IT WENT VIRAL!

IT'S ABOUT THAT IDIOT HARUTO.

WHAT DID YOU WANNA TALK ABOUT?

YEAH, YEAH, I KNOW.

OH, BUT DON'T GO CHASIN' AFTER MEN TOO MUCH, EITHER.

WE'RE ON THIN ICE RIGHT NOW.

eator Office BOOOOT

ON THAT NOTE, I'M GLAD I DON'T HAVE TO WORRY ABOUT YOU WITH WOMEN.

WASN'T THAT GREAT?!

OH YEAH, ABOUT THAT PROJECT!

THE BRAND COLLAB!

boys_run_the_riot

THEY GOT QUITE A FEW SALES AS WELL.

77
TS

1,349
FOLLOWE

oys_

pare

oysrunther...pees.net/

FOLLOWING

MESSAGE

I'M A BIG FAN OF THIS NEW BRAND

2020/04

05 RETWEETS 9216 LIKES

@wingchannel

@boys_run_the_riot
@wingchannel

ys_run_the_riot

IT GOT A LOT OF TRACTION ON SOCIAL MEDIA...

...AND BOYS RUN THE RIOT GOT A LOT OF FOLLOWERS, TOO!

!

NOW THEY CAN REPAY THE FAVOR.

THEY *OWE* US.

ALL OF YOUR CHANNEL'S TOPICS GO WELL...

...WITH A *TRANS HIGH SCHOOL BOY'S FASHION BRAND.*

WHAT DO YOU WANNA DO FOR YOUR NEXT PROJECT? FASHION? BEAUTY? LGBTQ STUFF?

WHAT DO YOU MEAN, *THEY OWE US?*

W...WAIT...

...INTERVIEWING RYO ON A DEEPER LEVEL?

HOW ABOUT ANOTHER VIDEO...

BESIDES, I THINK RYO'S ALREADY HAD ENOUGH...

THAT'S *NOT* WHY I DID A COLLAB WITH THEM.

THIS IS NOSTALGIC. REMINDS ME OF WHEN YOU FIRST CAME HERE...

WE'D ONLY JUST STARTED THE COMPANY.

LOOK AT YOU NOW. YOU'RE OUR BIGGEST EARNER.

YOU WERE SO SKINNY AND FRAIL, TOO.

...WHY BRING THAT UP ALL OF A SUDDEN?

YOU LEARNED IT FIRSTHAND.

WERE YOU CRITICIZED? NO.

YOU WERE SUPPORTED AND ACCEPTED. RIGHT?

EVERYONE KNOWS ABOUT LGBTQ STUFF NOW.

IT'S JUST ANOTHER PERSONAL TRAIT THESE DAYS.

TEACH THAT TO RYO.

IT'S A BREATH OF FRESH AIR...

...TO LIVE OPENLY AND HONESTLY LIKE THAT.

...

HEY!

ARE YOU BEING SARCASTIC?

...YOU HAVE SUCH A WAY WITH WORDS.

AS ALWAYS...

IF WE MAKE SOMETHING NEW, IT'LL PROBABLY SELL WELL.

...WHAT SHOULD WE DO?

EVEN IF WE START FROM SCRATCH...

WE'VE GOT A BUNCH OF NEW FOLLOWERS NOW.

SCUFF

THEY'RE JUST HERE TO FOLLOW A TREND, NOT TO BUY OUR STUFF.

THEY ONLY FOLLOWED US 'CUZ OF TSUBASA.

...I THINK WE SHOULD STOP CARIN' ABOUT THAT.

!

YEAH.

WHAT...? UH... D-DESIGN?!

YEAH, I GUESS...

BUT WHAT KIND OF RESEARCH?

WE NEED TO DO SOME MORE RESEARCH.

...EVEN IF NO ONE EXPECTS MUCH FROM US WITHOUT TSUBASA!

LET'S JUST MAKE LOTS OF STUFF...

WELL, MORE IMPORTANTLY, FIRST THINGS FIRST....

WE JUST HAVE TO GET MORE REAL FANS.

OBVIOUSLY A LOT MORE PEOPLE ARE WATCHING US NOW.

...AND GET THAT VIDEO REMOVED.

WE HAVE TO THANK TSUBASA...

IT SEEMS LIKE TSUBASA HAS A POLICY AROUND NOT DELETIN' VIDEOS.

THEY'VE ALREADY TURNED US DOWN ONCE BEFORE.

IT'S NOT GOING TO BE EASY.

ANYWAY, LET'S GO TO TSUBASA'S PLACE.

NO, KASHIWABARA SAID TSUBASA'S BEEN AT THE OFFICE SINCE THIS MORNING.

UGH... SERIOUSLY?

...THAT SUCKS. WHAT IF WE GIVE OUR EARNINGS BACK?

WE'RE THE ONES WHO PROPOSED THE IDEA FIRST...SO THAT'D ONLY BE FAIR.

HUH?

...I'LL CALL TSUBASA RIGHT NOW.

ABOUT THE NEXT PROJECT...

WHAT? THEN...THEY MUST BE TALKING ABOUT US ALREADY.

I'LL TALK TO TSUBASA.

WE'RE DOIN' THIS FOR *ME*.

I'M SURE...

...TSUBASA WILL UNDER-STAND HOW I FEEL.

BESIDES... I WANNA EXPLAIN IT PROPERLY.

TSUBASA

CALLING...

TSUBASA

WHAT'RE YOU CALLING ME FOR?

OH, RYO!

HELLO, TSUBASA?

BRRRRR... KER-CHAK

WHAT'S UP?

NO, IT'S FINE.

YOU BUSY?

SORRY TO BOTHER YOU.

I WANT YOU TO DELETE THAT VIDEO.

ACTUALLY, I HAVE A FAVOR TO ASK...

I DON'T WANNA BE OUT IN YOUR VIDEO AS A TRANSGENDER PERSON.

I DON'T WANNA LIE TO MYSELF...!

...I'M GONNA LIVE AS A GUY, SO...

I DECIDED THAT...

...I WANT MY STRENGTH TO COME FROM NOT GIVING UP ON MY IDEAL SELF.

...IF YOUR STRENGTH COMES FROM OUTING YOUR WHOLE PAST...

I ALREADY DELETED THAT VIDEO AGES AGO.

WE'RE NOT SIMILAR.

NOT ONE BIT.

TSUBAS

RYO.

WH...

WHY...?

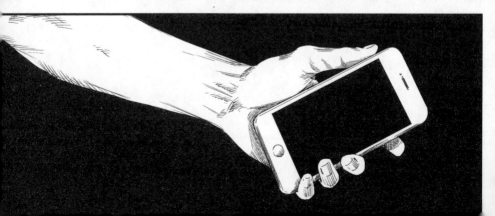

I DON'T WANNA LIE TO MYSELF...!

...I'M GONNA LIVE AS A GUY.

I DECIDED THAT...

Chap. 24 Betrayal

I... YEAH, YOU'RE RIGHT.

!

TSUBASA.

YOU'RE THE STAR OF THE PARTY, AREN'TCHA? WHY THE LONG FACE?

PAT

AFTER ALL, I'M THE YOUTUBER, WING!!

ALL RIGHT, GUESS WHO'S DRINKING TONIGHT?!

SMACK SMACK

I GOTTA SNAP OUT OF IT...

?

...

REX

?

WING-KUN.

HUH?

HEY... LOOK AT THIS.

...! HEY, BOSS...

WE'RE ALL HERE, RIGHT? OH, TSUBASA!

THIS IS THE PRICE YOU PAY FOR FAME, HUH? JEEZ...

VRRR VRRR

I KEEP GETTIN' CALLS ABOUT THIS SHITTY RUMOR. OH, HERE'S ANOTHER ONE...

RIGHT, TSUBASA? HEY...

AM I RIGHT?

IT'S *TSUBASA*.

MUTTER

WHY WOULD TSUBASA SLEEP WITH A FAN? LET ALONE A WOMAN?

HEY, NO ONE PAY IT ANY MIND. IT COULDN'T BE TRUE.

MUTTER

MUTTER

...SAY SOMETHIN', DAMMIT!!

WHAT'S GOING ON HERE?

WHAT'S WITH YOU?

...

...AND CASHING IN ON IT?

HAVE YOU BEEN PRETENDING ALL THIS TIME...

...!! N...NO...

WAS THIS ALL A LIE?

DID YOU JUST MAKE UP A PERSONA?

I BET YOU PRETENDED YOUR LIFE WAS SOME TRAGEDY TO GARNER SYMPATHY, FAME, AND STATUS, AND THEN WENT AND SCREWED A WOMAN BEHIND THE SCENES.

NO TO *WHAT?*

...WELL, AREN'T YOU JUST A PIECE OF TRASH.

THIS IS THE FIRST TIME...

...I'VE EVER FELT SO BETRAYED.

SWAY...

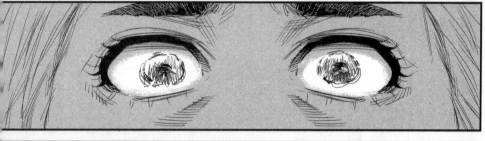

DASH

TSUBASA-CHAN!

...HOW DID THINGS END UP LIKE THIS?

EVEN I DON'T UNDER-STAND.

Venting of a high school boy who was bullied as a "sissy" at school, episode 35

8,535 views

106 Comments

i wanna be your friend XD

👍 5   👎   Reply

BOOOOT Corporation CEO   1 day ago

I'd love to make videos with you.
If you'd like, we could make some fun
content together.
Please get in touch!!

XXOO@email.com

bttp://www.boooot.cow/

👍   👎   Reply

Mao   1 day ago

i can't wait for tomorrow!

...AND I LEARNED NEW THINGS ABOUT MYSELF.

"I TRY TO BE EVEN MORE FEMININE AND MORE BEAUTIFUL THAN WOMEN."

THAT'S WHAT WING REPRE-SENTED...

"I'M GAY, BUT I HATE WHAT THAT MEANS FOR MY FUTURE."

...HOW COULD I DO THAT?!

SO...

THAT'S NOT WHO WING IS.

THAT'S NOT WHO WING IS...

...I'D JUST GO BACK TO BEING ALONE—

BUT IF I'M NOT WING...

Chap. 25 Irresponsible

TSUBASA...!!

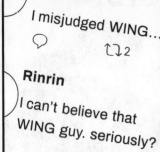

Inagawa

I misjudged WING...

💬   ↻2

Rinrin

I can't believe that WING guy. seriously?

💬1

433

A photo of the YouTuber WING sleeping with a fan has caused quite a stir. WING has a very effeminate persona and often talks about not being attracted to women in videos. Many are enraged by the prospect that WING has been falsifying being a member of the LGBTQ community to fool fans, causing a huge backlash.

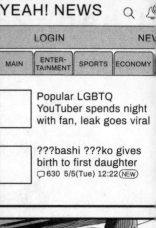

Popular LGBTQ YouTuber spends night with fan, leak goes viral

???bashi ???ko gives birth to first daughter
💬630 5/5(Tue) 12:22 (NEW)

...WHAT ARE YOU GONNA DO, TSUBASA?

IN THAT CASE...

...THAT'S THE INTERNET FOR YOU.

WHAT'S WITH THESE PEOPLE...? THEY JUST SAY ANY OLD SHIT.

APOLOGIZE FOR WHAT?

YOUR... IMAGE.

THAT SHOULD HELP MY IMAGE.

I'LL RELEASE AN APOLOGY VIDEO.

THEY SAY YOU MADE UP YOUR ENTIRE PAST AND YOUR UPBRINGING...

ARE YOU GONNA ADMIT TO LYING, LIKE THE RUMOR SAYS?

...

...I REALLY LOST MY UNDER-STANDING OF WHO I AM.

...WHILE I WAS WORKING AS WING...

I WASN'T *LYING*... BUT...

THIS ISN'T LIKE YOU!

...AND THE VOICES OF THOSE AROUND YOU.

ISN'T *THAT* WHO YOU ARE, TSUBASA?

YOU FIGHT FOR YOUR-SELF...

...YOU DON'T GET IT, DO YOU?

YOU COULD DESCRIBE YOURSELF *THAT* WAY...

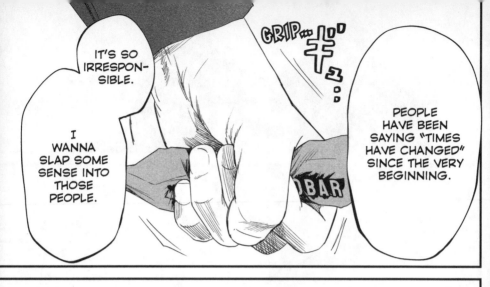

HERE'S SOME SWEETS AND STUFF FROM US, AS THANKS FOR THE VIDEO!

WELL... ANYWAY, TAKE A BREAK AND RELAX FOR NOW.

...

!

IT'S ONE OF YUTAKA'S FAVORITES...

...OH. I RECOGNIZE THIS CHOCOLATE.

TOPIC

Saya
Replying to
i don't know
much about this
WING person but i
hate them already lol

♡

San @A_Oji_Xh
i can't believe this thing with
WING. Anyone who defends
him is disgusting

♡

sho @riO3_XiiO
Thanks to WING, people a
going to lump all LGBT
people together.
This is awful.

...IS THERE?

THERE'S...

...NOTHING
WE CAN DO...

DO WE
JUST HAVE
TO SIT AND
WATCH...

...UNTIL
THIS ALL
WASHES
OVER...?

WE
BORROWED
TSUBASA'S
POPULARITY
TO SELL OUR
STUFF.

...I HAVE...

...AN IDEA.

BOYS RUN
ボーイズ・ラン・ザ・ライオット
THE RIOT

BOYS RUN

ボーイズ・ラン・ザ・ライオット

THE RIOT

Chap. 26 Character

...YOU'RE MORE *GENDERFLUID*, RIGHT?

SINCE YOUR GENDER CAN SOMETIMES CHANGE AND STUFF.

THERE'S ALL KINDS OF NONBINARY GENDERS, LIKE GENDER NEUTRAL, BIGENDER, AND AGENDER, BUT IN YOUR CASE...

I FIRST LEARNED ABOUT YOU...

...DO YOU KNOW ALL THAT...?

H-HOW...

...WHEN WE WERE LITTLE.

...WHEN MY PARENTS TOLD ME...

BUT I STUDIED STUFF ON MY OWN, TOO.

THEY JUST DON'T *UNDER-STAND*...

LIKE *I* DIDN'T.

BUT MOST PEOPLE DON'T *HATE* YOU.

THERE ARE SOME IDIOTS OUT THERE WHO WILL MESS WITH YOU AND HURT YOU.

SO... DON'T JUST GO OFF ON YOUR OWN.

I THINK PEOPLE *WANT* TO LEARN.

UH-HUH.

...HUH?

...WELL THEN, SHALL WE GET EDITING?

Chusa
Have you heard about this, Tsubasa-kun?
ht*p://ins*/boysruntheriot

👍 43 👎   Reply

ryo
Those are the guys who collabed with WING. I couldn't believe it when I saw it too. Looks like they did a collab.
👍 4 👎   Reply

Chan
I saw it. They're really fanning the damn flames lmao
They're just getting carried away cuz WING's getting them sales
👍 3 👎   Reply

...WHAT?

THAT'S BOYS RUN THE RIOT'S ACCOUNT....

...HUH?

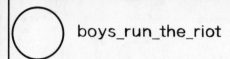 boys_run_the_riot

Liked by chidschikl8t and others

boys_run_the_riot wing T-shirt

View all 22 comments

IT'S IN ENGLISH.

...WHAT IS THIS?

...THAT'S WHAT IT MEANS.

"NONE OF OUR BUSINESS."

IS THIS BASED ON THE STORY I TOLD THEM ABOUT YUTAKA...?

THAT'S NONE OF MY BUSINESS.

...HEH.

?

WHAT A ROUNDABOUT WAY TO SAY IT.

THEY'RE TOO COOL FOR THEIR OWN GOOD.

IT'S NO ONE'S BUSINESS...

EVEN OURS.

boys_run_the_riot

None of our business

Liked by chidschiki8t and others
boys_run_the_riot wing T-shirt
View all 22 comments

"NONE OF OUR BUSINESS."

HOW SCARY...

I KNOW, RIGHT?

...YIKES. LOOK AT THESE HATE COMMENTS.

...WHEN THEY'RE DROWNIN'.

YOU'RE NOT HELPIN' JUST BY HIGH-FIVIN' SOMEONE...

HEHEH.

HUH? 'COURSE I'M NOT.

ARE YOU LISTENING?! ARE YOU EVEN WORKING?!

JOE-SAN!

JOE-SAN.

WE GOT A CALL FROM A CLIENT THIS EVENING—

To be continued in volume 4

SPECIAL THANKS

CONTRIBUTORS

Artist: knott aka 2G INDAHOUSE (Instagram: knott2g)

Art director: SAYAKA (Twitter/Instagram: @SAYAKACHAN)
(Chap. 21 Border, from page 86)

STAFF

Igarashi
Ryuusei Terada
Taiga Miyahara

SPECIAL VOLUME DESIGN

fake graphics – Akito Sumiyoshi

EDITORS

Hidemi Shiraki
Haruhito Uwai

SPECIAL VOLUME EDITORS

Tomohiro Ebitani
The Young Magazine editorial team

TRANSLATION NOTES

GYARU, page 32
Gyaru, though initially borrowed from the English term "girl" and "gal", has since become a subculture of Japanese street fashion. *Gyaru* typically bleach and dye their hair lighter, wear a lot of make-up and gaudy accessories, and often tan their skin. *Gyaru* are considered to be cheerful, sociable, and trendy, but, because of their appearance, are also sometimes thought of as vain, shallow, or airheaded.

CROSSDRESSER, page 159
In the original Japanese, this character is asking if Tsubasa is an *onee*. *Onee* literally means "big sister." It can be used for anyone assigned male at birth who acts or looks effeminate, so it can encompass effeminate gay men, crossdressers, drag queens, transgender women, and transfeminine people. Some people do not like being called *onee*, but some people do, and even self-identify as *onee*.

X-GENDER, page 175
X-gender is a Japanese term for a gender identity that is neither male nor female, and is similar to the terms "nonbinary" and "genderqueer" in English. The term x-gender is often used both on its own as its own gender identity and as an umbrella term for various nonbinary genders (See translation note below).

NONBINARY, GENDER NEUTRAL, BIGENDER, AGENDER, GENDERFLUID, page 176
The gender identities Kashiwabara lists here all fall under the nonbinary umbrella, and are gender identities that exist outside of the gender binary—meaning that they refer to genders that are neither male nor female. "Nonbinary" refers to a gender that is neither strictly male nor female, and can be used both on its own as its own gender identity, and as an umbrella term for various nonbinary genders; "Gender neutral" refers to someone with a neutral gender identity or expression; "Bigender" refers to someone who identifies as two different genders, either simultaneously or by fluctuating between the two; "Agender" refers to someone who does not identify as any particular gender; and "Genderfluid" refers to someone whose gender identity may shift between different genders at different times, or in different circumstances.

GAKURAN, page 191
Here, and more clearly on the cover image, we see Tsubasa wearing a *gakuran*, or a type of traditional Japanese male school uniform. *Gakuran* are typically worn by middle school and high school boys, and are normally all black or navy blue. A *gakuran* consists of a button-down top with a standing collar, and straight-leg slacks.

BOYS RUN THE RIOT VOLUME 3
ORIGINAL U.S. COVER SKETCH
BY AUTHOR KEITO GAKU

PERFECT WORLD

Rie Aruga

A TOUCHING
NEW SERIES
ABOUT LOVE AND
COPING WITH
DISABILITY

An office party reunites Tsugumi with her high school crush Itsuki. He's realized his dream of becoming an architect, but along the way, he experienced a spinal injury that put him in a wheelchair. Now Tsugumi's rekindled feelings will butt up against prejudices she never considered — and Itsuki will have to decide if he's ready to let someone into his heart...

KC
KODANSHA
COMICS

Knight of the Ice ©Yayoi Ogawa/Kodansha Ltd.

SKATING THRILLS AND ICY CHILLS WITH THIS NEW TINGLY ROMANCE SERIES!

A rom-com on ice, perfect for fans of *Princess Jellyfish* and *Wotakoi*. Kokoro is the talk of the figure-skating world, winning trophies and hearts. But little do they know... he's actually a huge nerd! From the beloved creator of *You're My Pet* (*Tramps Like Us*).

Chitose is a serious young woman, working for the health magazine *SASSO*. Or at least, she would be, if she wasn't constantly getting distracted by her childhood friend, international figure skating star Kokoro Kijinami! In the public eye and on the ice, Kokoro is a gallant, flawless knight, but behind his glittery costumes and breathtaking spins lies a secret: He's actually a hopelessly romantic otaku, who can only land his quad jumps when Chitose is on hand to recite a spell from his favorite magical girl anime!

KC/ KODANSHA COMICS

The adorable new odd-couple cat comedy manga from the creator of the beloved *Chi's Sweet Home*, in full color!

Praise for Chi's Sweet Home

"Nearly impossible to turn away... a true all-ages title that anyone, young or old, cat lover or not, will enjoy. The stories will bring a smile to your face and warm your heart."

—*School Library Journal*

Sue & Tai-chan

Konami Kanata

Sue is an aging housecat who's looking forward to living out her life in peace... but her plans change when the mischievous black tomcat Tai-chan enters the picture! Hey! Sue never signed up to be a catsitter! *Sue & Tai-chan* is the latest from the reigning meow-narch of cute kitty comics, Konami Kanata.

Young characters and steampunk setting, like *Howl's Moving Castle* and *Battle Angel Alita*

Beyond the Clouds © 2018 Nicke / Ki-oon

A boy with a talent for machines and a mysterious girl whose wings he's fixed will take you beyond the clouds! In the tradition of the high-flying, resonant adventure stories of Studio Ghibli comes a gorgeous tale about the longing of young hearts for adventure and friendship!

THE WORLD OF CLAMP!

Cardcaptor Sakura
Collector's Edition

Cardcaptor Sakura:
Clear Card

Magic Knight Rayearth
25th Anniversary Box Set

Chobits

TSUBASA Omnibus

TSUBASA WoRLD CHRoNiCLE

xxxHOLiC Omnibus

xxxHOLiC Rei

CLOVER Collector's Edition

Kodansha Comics welcomes you to explore the expansive world of CLAMP, the all-female artist collective that has produced some of the most acclaimed manga of the century. Our growing catalog includes icons like *Cardcaptor Sakura* and *Magic Knight Rayearth*, each crafted with CLAMP's one-of-a-kind style and characters!

The beloved characters from *Cardcaptor Sakura* return in a brand new, reimagined fantasy adventure!

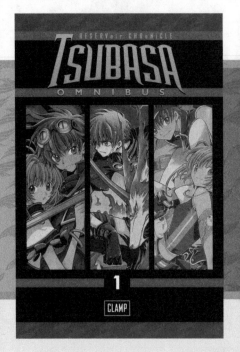

"[*Tsubasa*] takes readers on a fantastic ride that only gets more exhilarating with each successive chapter." —Anime News Network

In the Kingdom of Clow, an archaeological dig unleashes an incredible power, causing Princess Sakura to lose her memories. To save her, her childhood friend Syaoran must follow the orders of the Dimension Witch and travel alongside Kurogane, an unrivaled warrior; Fai, a powerful magician; and Mokona, a curiously strange creature, to retrieve Sakura's dispersed memories!

MAGIC KNIGHT RAYEARTH
25TH ANNIVERSARY EDITION
CLAMP

A BELOVED CLASSIC MAKES ITS STUNNING RETURN IN THIS GORGEOUS, LIMITED EDITION BOX SET!

This tale of three Tokyo teenagers who cross through a magical portal and become the champions of another world is a modern manga classic. The box set includes three volumes of manga covering the entire first series of *Magic Knight Rayearth*, plus the series's super-rare full-color art book companion, all printed at a larger size than ever before on premium paper, featuring a newly-revised translation and lettering, and exquisite foil-stamped covers. A strictly limited edition, this will be gone in a flash!

Something's Wrong With Us

NATSUMI ANDO

The dark, psychological, sexy shojo series readers have been waiting for!

A spine-chilling and steamy romance between a Japanese sweets maker and the man who framed her mother for murder!

Following in her mother's footsteps, Nao became a traditional Japanese sweets maker, and with unparalleled artistry and a bright attitude, she gets an offer to work at a world-class confectionary company. But when she meets the young, handsome owner, she recognizes his cold stare...

KC
KODANSHA
COMICS

A SMART, NEW ROMANTIC COMEDY FOR FANS OF *SHORTCAKE CAKE* AND *TERRACE HOUSE*!

A romance manga starring high school girl Meeko, who learns to live on her own in a boarding house whose living room is home to the odd (but handsome) Matsunaga-san. She begins to adjust to her new life away from her parents, but Meeko soon learns that no matter how far away from home she is, she's still a young girl at heart — especially when she finds herself falling for Matsunaga-san.

"Clever, sassy, and original....*xxxHOLiC* has the inherent hallmarks of a runaway hit."
—NewType magazine

Beautifully seductive artwork and uniquely Japanese depictions of the supernatural will hypnotize CLAMP fans!

Kimihiro Watanuki is haunted by visions of ghosts and spirits. He seeks help from a mysterious woman named Yuko, who claims she can help. However, Watanuki must work for Yuko in order to pay for her aid. Soon Watanuki finds himself employed in Yuko's shop, where he sees things and meets customers that are stranger than anything he could have ever imagined.

KC
KODANSHA COMICS

The boys are back, in 400-page hardcovers that are as pretty and badass as they are!

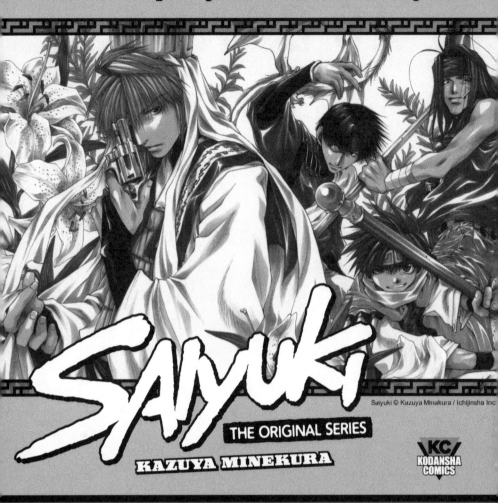

Saiyuki © Kazuya Minakura / Ichijinsha Inc

SAIYUKI

THE ORIGINAL SERIES

KAZUYA MINEKURA

KC/ KODANSHA COMICS

"AN EDGY COMIC LOOK AT AN ANCIENT CHINESE TALE." —YALSA

Genjo Sanzo is a Buddhist priest in the city of Togenkyo, which is being ravaged by yokai spirits that have fallen out of balance with the natural order. His superiors send him on a journey far to the west to discover why this is happening and how to stop it. His companions are three yokai with human souls. But this is no day trip — the four will encounter many discoveries and horrors on the way.

FEATURES NEW TRANSLATION, COLOR PAGES, AND BEAUTIFUL WRAPAROUND COVER ART!

The slow-burn queer romance that'll sweep you off your feet!

10 DANCE

Inouesatoh presents

"A FANTASTIC DEBUT VOLUME… ONE OF MY FAVORITE BOOKS OF THE YEAR…"
— AiPT!

"10 DANCE IS A MUST-READ FOR ANYONE WHO'S ENJOYED MANGA AND ANIME ABOUT COMPETITIVE DANCE (ON OR OFF THE ICE!)."
—Anime UK News

Shinya Sugiki, the dashing lord of Standard Ballroom, and Shinya Suzuki, passionate king of Latin Dance: The two share more than just a first name and a love of the sport. They each want to become champion of the 10-Dance Competition, which means they'll need to learn the other's specialty dances, and who better to learn from than the best? But old rivalries die hard, and things get further complicated when they realize there might be more between them than an uneasy partnership...

KC KODANSHA COMICS

ANIME OUT NOW FROM SENTAI FILMWORKS!

A BL romance between a good boy who didn't know he was waiting for a hero, and a bad boy who comes to his rescue!

Masahiro Setagawa doesn't believe in heroes, but wishes he could: He's found himself in a gang of small-time street bullies, and with no prospects for a real future. But when high school teacher (and scourge of the streets) Kousuke Ohshiba comes to his rescue, he finds he may need to start believing after all... in heroes, and in his budding feelings, too.

Hitorijime My Hero

Memeco Arii

KC KODANSHA COMICS

Chobits © CLAMP-ShigatsuTsuitachi CO.,LTD./Kodansha Ltd.

THE SWEET SCENT OF LOVE IS IN THE AIR! FOR FANS OF OFFBEAT ROMANCES LIKE *WOTAKOI*

Sweat and Soap © Kintetsu Yamada / Kodansha Ltd.

In an office romance, there's a fine line between sexy and awkward... and that line is where Asako — a woman who sweats copiously — meets Koutarou — a perfume developer who can't get enough of Asako's, er, scent. Don't miss a romcom manga like no other!

KC
KODANSHA
COMICS

A Kodansha Comics Trade Paperback Original
Boys Run the Riot 3 copyright © 2020 Keito Gaku
English translation copyright © 2021 Keito Gaku

All rights reserved.

Published in the United States by Kodansha Comics, an imprint of Kodansha USA Publishing, LLC, New York.

Publication rights for this English edition arranged through Kodansha Ltd., Tokyo.

First published in Japan in 2020 by Kodansha Ltd., Tokyo as *Boys Run the Riot*, volume 3.

ISBN 978-1-64651-119-8

Printed in the United States of America.

www.kodansha.us

9 8 7 6 5 4 3 2 1
Translation: Leo McDonagh
Lettering: Ashley Caswell
Editing: Tiff Joshua TJ Ferentini
Kodansha Comics edition cover design by Phil Balsman

Publisher: Kiichiro Sugawara

Director of publishing services: Ben Applegate
Associate director of operations: Stephen Pakula
Publishing services managing editors: Alanna Ruse, Madison Salters
Assistant production managers: Emi Lotto, Angela Zurlo
Logo and character art ©Kodansha USA Publishing, LLC